AN INTRODUCTION TO

PLAYING BOOGIE, BLUES & JAZZ

A FIRST REPERTORY FOR EARLY-GRADE PIANISTS
SELECTED AND EDITED BY
DENES AGAY

Order No. YK 21734
US International Standard Book Number: 0.8256.8093.X
UK International Standard Book Number: 0.7119.6116.6

Yorktown Music Press, Inc.

HAL•LEONARD®
7777 W. BLUEMOUND RD. P.O. BOX 13819 MILWAUKEE, WI 53213

CONTENTS

BOOGIE PATTERNS

- The essence of boogie is an ever-recurring bass pattern, a usually lively "basso ostinato" providing a solid rhythmic background for a strongly punctuated right hand melody.

Below is a progressive listing of bass figures in the boogie vein. Each pattern should be practiced in a I-IV-V-I (tonic-subdominant-dominant-tonic) chord sequence, repeating once each measure. Also, each sequence should be transposed to one or two other suitable keys, in which the shifting patterns lie easily under the hands. (All ♫♫ patterns can also be played ♪ ♫♪ .)

Skip to My Boogie

Lively

Gerald Martin

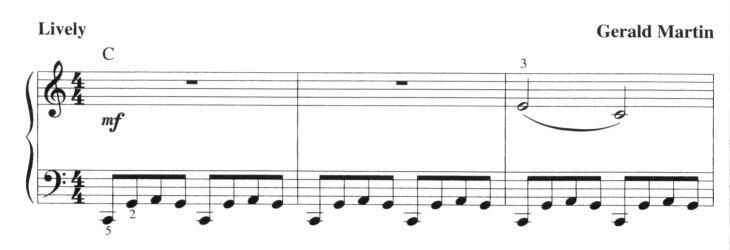

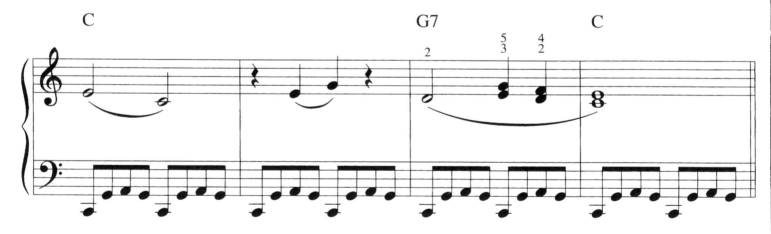

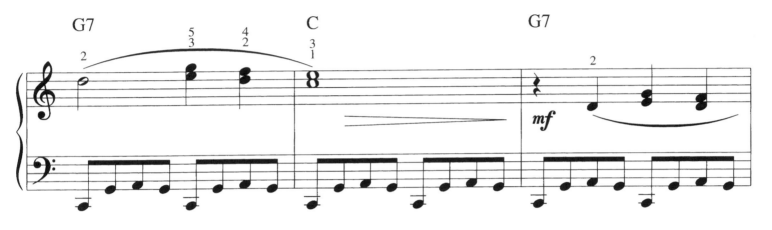

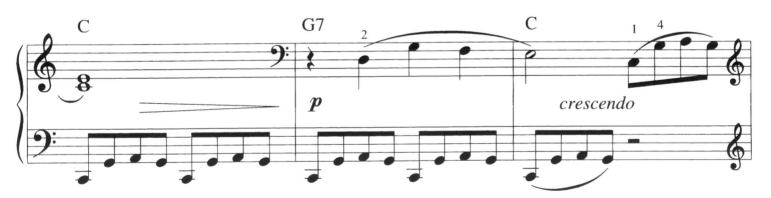

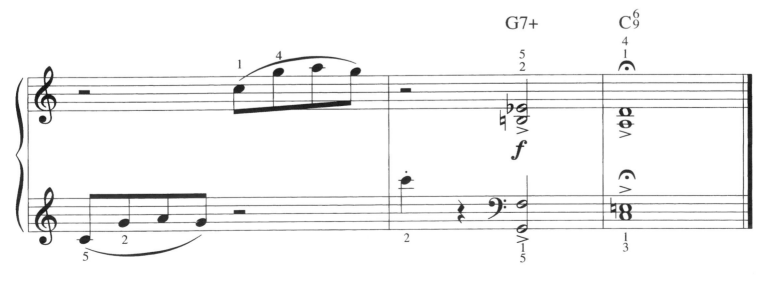

The Little Boogie Man

Moderately lively

Denes Agay

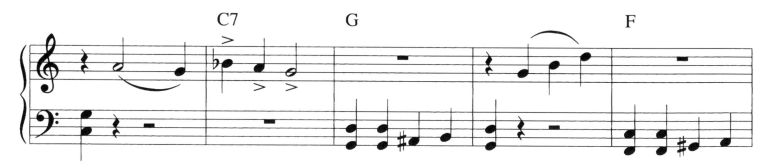

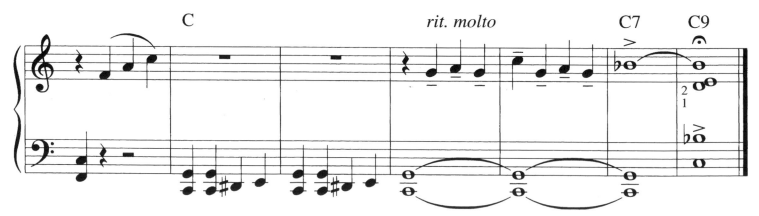

- The earliest traditional blues form is built on a harmonic sequence of 12 measures, divided into three phrases, with a freely improvised expressive melody line.

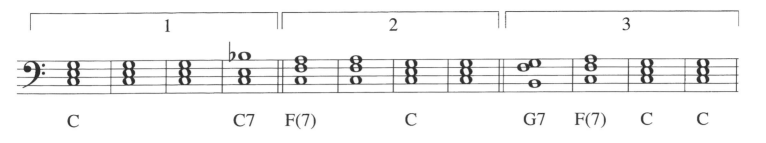

- This sequence is not rigid, of course; harmonic shifts, melodic and rhythmic embellishments occur very often.

The Easy Rider Blues

With a slow beat

Traditional

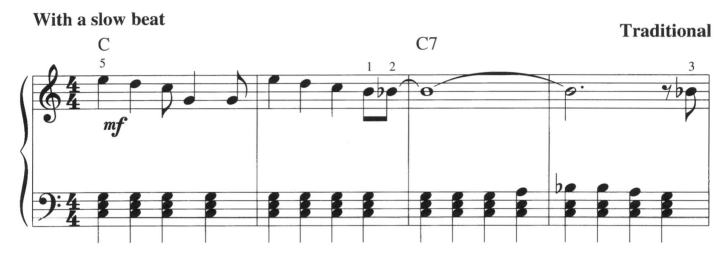

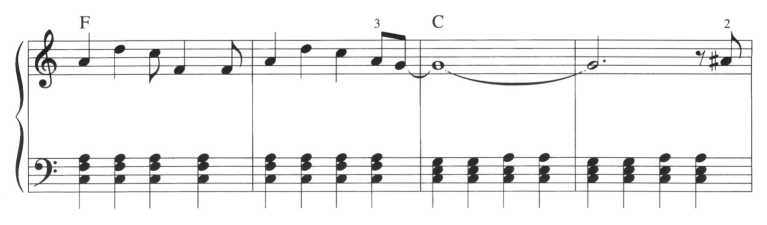

Warm-up Boogie

Moderato

Gerald Martin

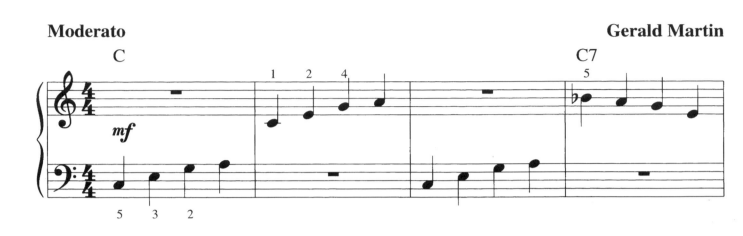

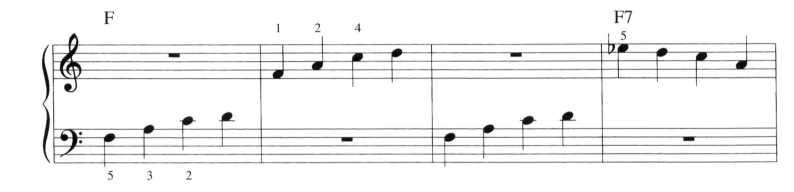

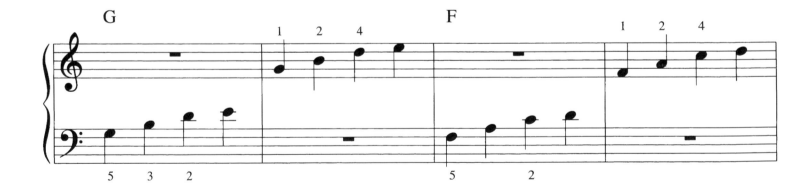

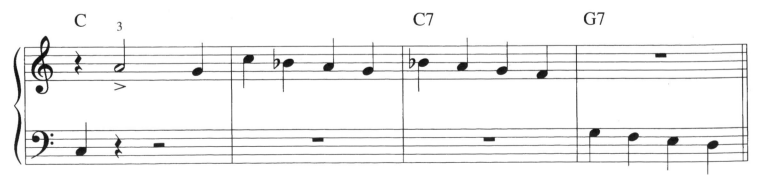

(same tempo)

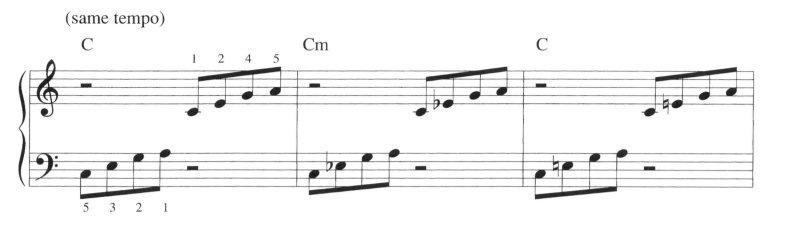

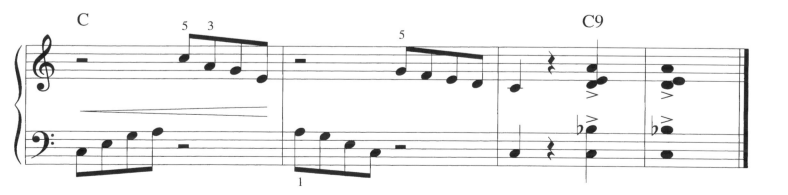

Just Plain Blue

Slowly, with a heavy beat

Denes Agay

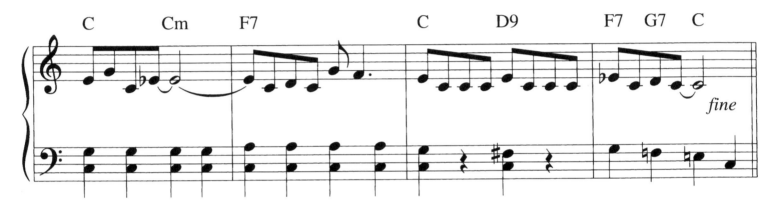

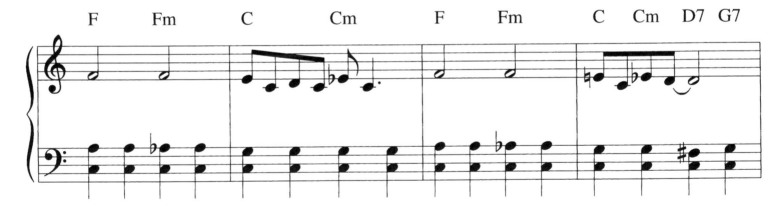

Five Finger Stomp

Medium bounce

Denes Agay

Careless Love Boogie

Moderately bright

Traditional

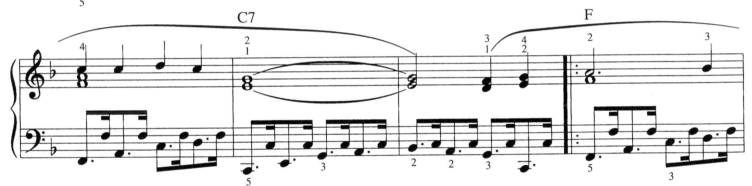

The Boll Weevil Boogie

Moderately

Folk Tune

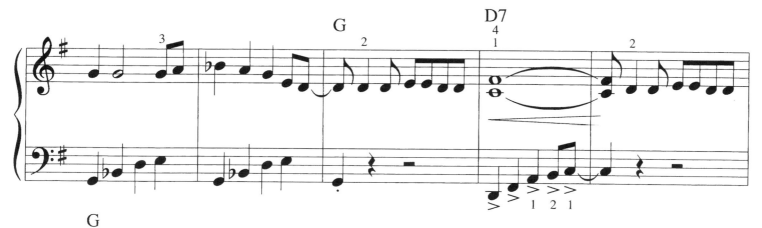

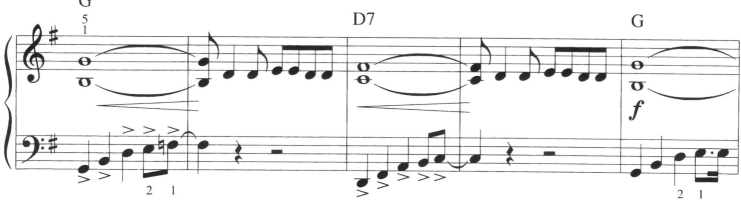

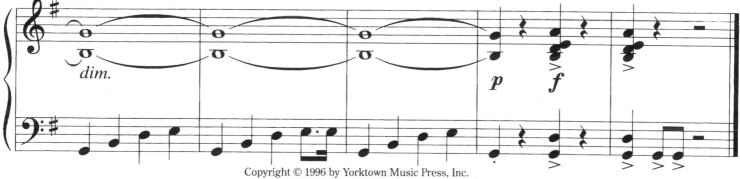

The Darktown Strutters

Moderately with a strong beat

S. Brooks

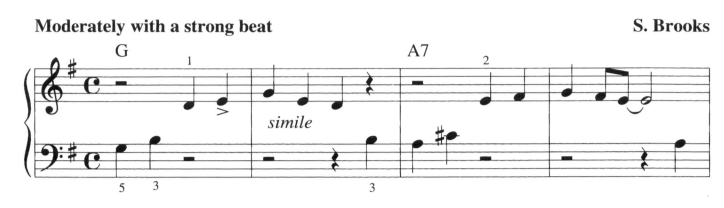

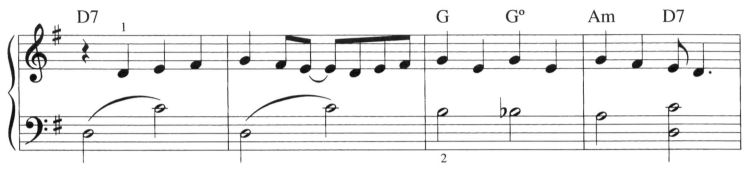

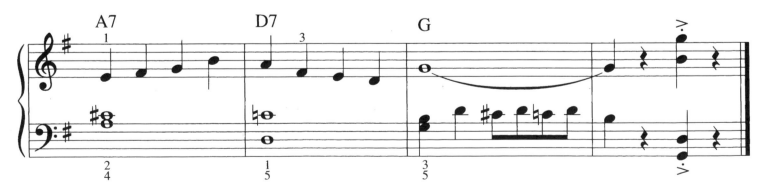

Lazy Afternoon

Moderately slow

Denes Agay

Whistle-Stop Boogie

Steady beat (moderate to brisk)

Gerald Martin

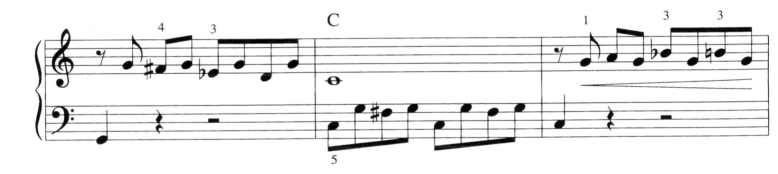

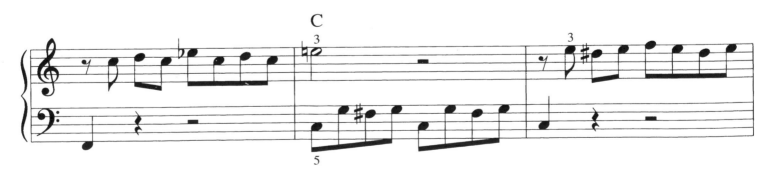

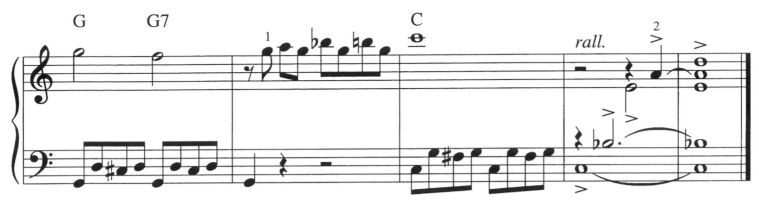

Rock-A My Soul

Lively bounce

Spiritual

Harmony Rag

Moderately

Hal Nichols

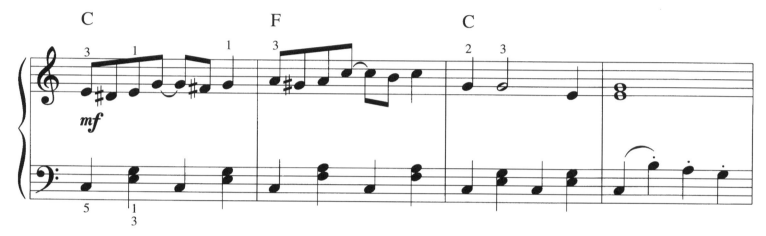

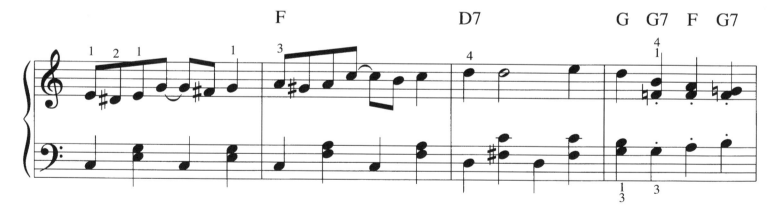

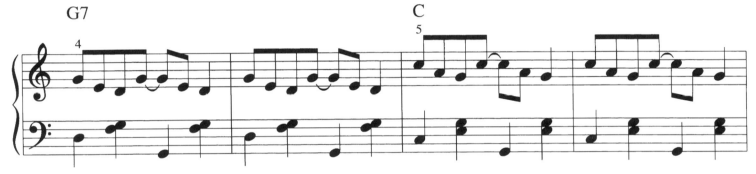

Whistling the Blues

Slowly drifting

Denes Agay

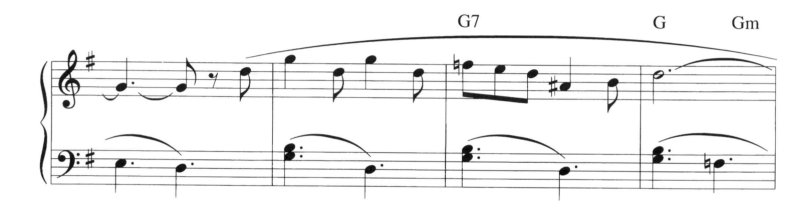

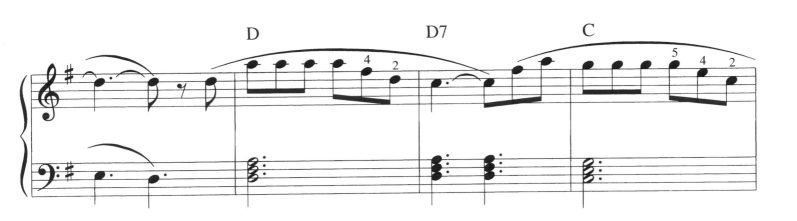

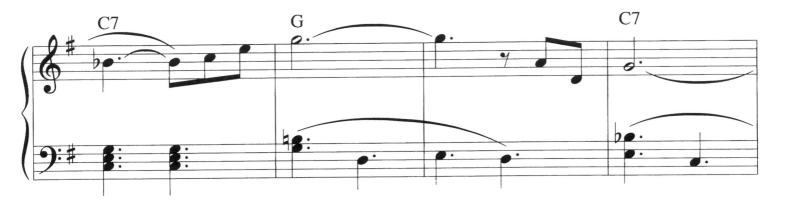

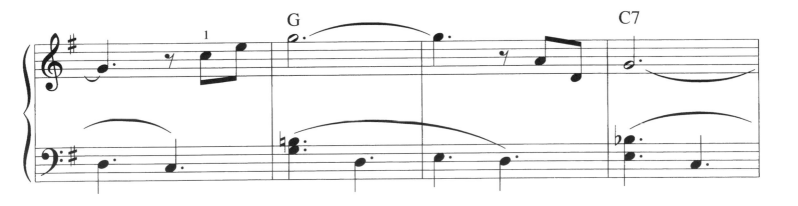

Valsette en Bleu

Moderato con grazia

Denes Agay

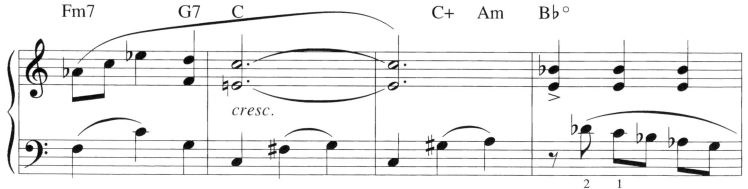

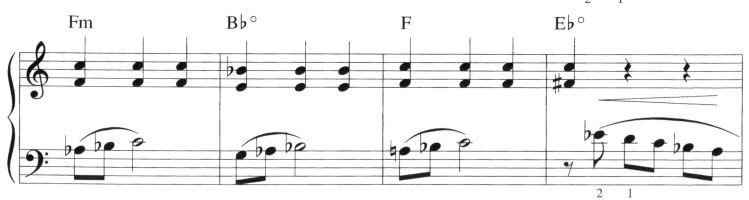

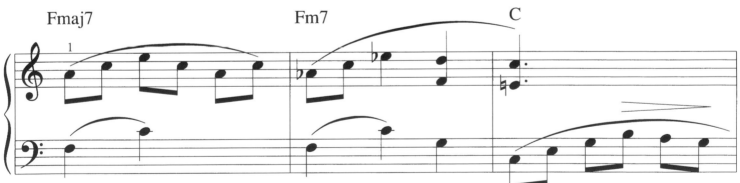

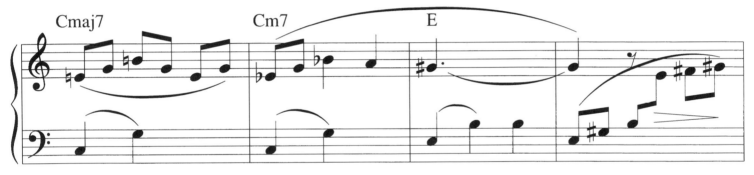

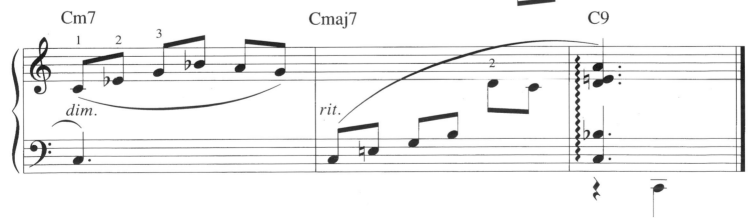

Sailor's Boogie

Very lively

Gerald Martin

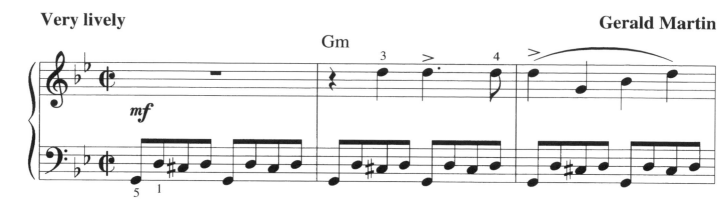

BITS OF JAZZ—STEP BY STEP

- The heart of jazz is improvisation, an on-the-spur-of-the-moment shaping and molding of the underlying musical elements.
- The characteristic sound of jazz is given not so much by what is played, but by how it is played.
- The most important basic trait of jazz is a steady pronounced beat, a steady metric pulse underlying and supporting the entire structure of musical manipulations. This pulse should be felt and implied even under long-held notes and chords. In the beginning, and even later on, light tapping of the beat units with the right foot (heel on the floor) will help maintain and emphasize the metric momentum.
- There is a wide choice of suitable, appealing materials among the many well-known folk songs, play tunes, nursery rhymes which can be used by the early-grade pianist for a progressive exploration of the jazz idiom. The following variations of "London Bridge" may furnish some ideas how these traditional simple melodies can furnish a tentative plan.
- At every step of the way the player should feel free and encouraged to make up individual versions of the same tune. Naturally, only those patterns and variants given here should be used which are consistent with the player's grade level and native skill.

London Bridge
(Progressive Variations)

Traditional

Play it "straight" at first with a pronounced beat. Tap the beat units with your foot, or with the left hand on the piano.

- Provide the melody with a simple bass. Play at first without the melody, with a good beat, then add the tune in the right hand.

- Arrange the melody notes into a syncopated pattern. Play it at first with the right hand only (tapping the beat), then add the bass (which is the same as in the preceding examples).

- Try this more interesting variant of the melody, with some changes in the bass, too. The hornpipe pattern (♪♪) occurs very often in jazz.

- Melody in thirds with a "walking bass":

- Another version, with the simplest ostinato boogie pattern in the bass:

Lively

- For a more modern harmonization of the melody, try this step-by-step sequence of diatonic seventh chords (you may play it first by omitting the top notes of the left hand chords).

- Keeping the same chord progression in the left hand, the melody may be varied in many ways. Play this version and also invent one or two others.

- From ragtime to modern jazz, a commonly used accompaniment pattern is the familiar "oom-pah" formula, variously called "swing bass" or "stride bass." (The middle voice in the right hand is optional.)

Walking tempo

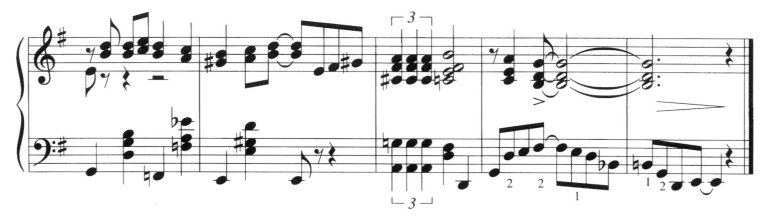

- The innumerable variation possibilities inherent in a good tune can take the jazz player as far afield as imagination and ingenuity allows. The following "ballad" version varies all elements of the theme and retains only the form (phrasing) structure. (Slight alterations of the melody's rhythm pattern are possible: ♩♪♩♪♩♪ or ♩♪♪♪♪)

Moderato

- Another version in a "rock and roll" vein. The most conspicuous trait of this style is the placing of accents on the second and fourth beats, instead of the normally accented first and third beats. There is also a frequent use of triplets with a pronounced metric pulse on the eighth-notes.

Moderately lively

Rock and Roll Smoky

Moderately

Gerald Martin

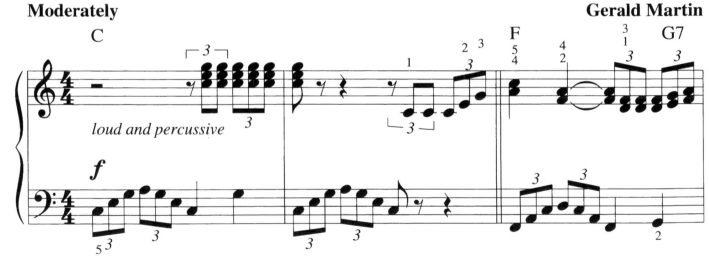

loud and percussive

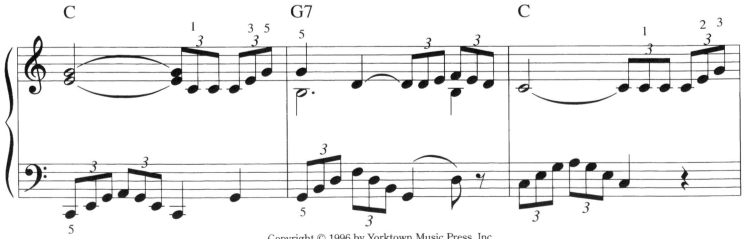

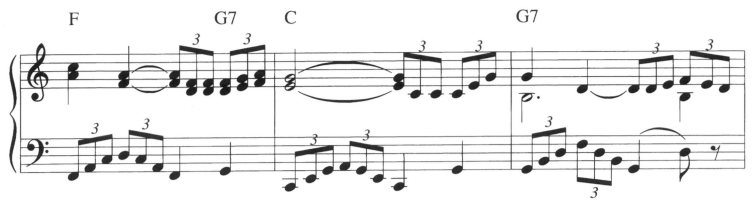

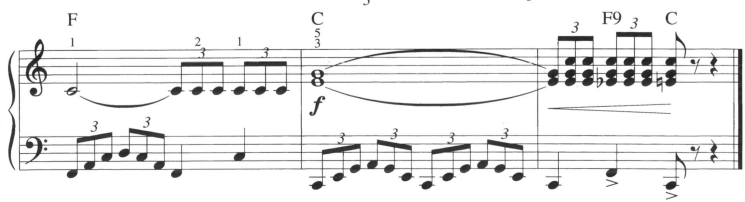

Little Brown Jug

Medium bounce

Traditional

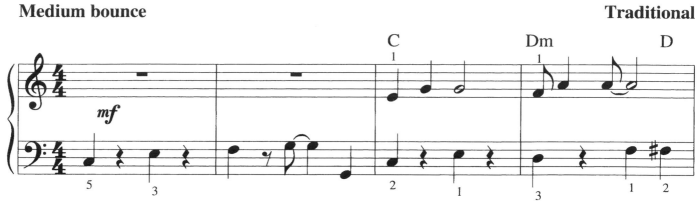

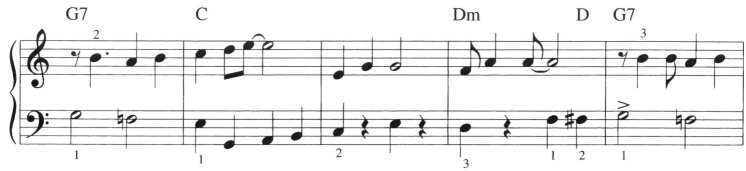

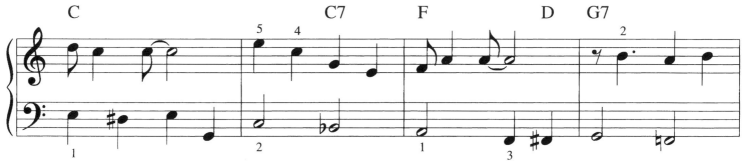

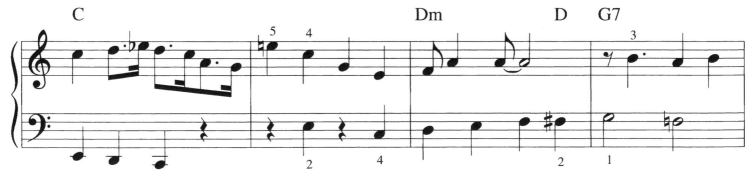